TAGORE

TAGORE ON GANDHI

Rabindranath Tagore

Rupa & Co

Concept and Typeset Copyright © Rupa & Co. 2008

Published 2008 by
Rupa & Co
7/16, Ansari Road, Daryaganj,
New Delhi 110 002

Sales Centres:

Allahabad Bangalooru Chandigarh Chennai
Hyderabad Jaipur Kathmandu
Kolkata Mumbai Pune

All rights reserved.
No part of this publication may be reproduced, stored in a retrieval system, or transmitted, in any form or by any means, electronic, mechanical, photocopying, recording or otherwise, without the prior permission of the publishers.

Typeset by
Mindways Design
1410 Chiranjiv Tower
43 Nehru Place
New Delhi 110 019

Printed in India by
Gopsons Papers Ltd.
A-14 Sector 60
Noida 201 301

Contents

Gandhi Maharaj	1
A Liberated Soul	3
The Supreme Man	6
Mahatma Gandhi	8
Gandhi the Man	19
Mohandas Karamchand Gandhi	26
20 September	33
With Mahatmaji in Poona	40
On Mahatmaji's Birthday	51
Moral Warfare	55
References	57

Gandhi Maharaj

We who follow Gandhi Maharaja's lead
have one thing in common among us:
    we never fill our purses with spoils from
the poor nor bend our knees to the rich.

When they come bullying us
with raised fist and menacing sticks,
    we smile to them, and say:
your reddening stare
    may startle babies out of sleep,
but how frighten those who refuse to fear?

Our speeches are straight and simple,
no diplomatic turns to twist their meaning;
    confounding penal code

they guide with perfect ease the pilgrims
   to the border of jail.

And when these crowd the path to the prison gate,
   their stains of insult are washed clean,
their age-long shackles drop to the dust,
   and on their forehead are stamped
Gandhiji's blessings.

15 February 1940

A Liberated Soul

'What do you think of Mahatma Gandhi?'

'What do I think of Mahatma Gandhi?' said the poet-philosopher, emphatically. 'Why, I think very highly of Gandhi. He is a great man, a great soul. He, today, wields tremendous power over the teeming millions of India.'

'What is really the secret of his success?'

'The secret of Gandhiji's success lies in his dynamic spiritual strength and incessant self-sacrifice. Many public men make sacrifices for selfish reasons. It is a sort of investment that yields handsome dividends. Gandhi is altogether different. He is unique in his nobility. His very life is another name for sacrifice. He is sacrifice itself. He covets no power, no position, no wealth, no name and no fame. Offer him the throne of all India, he will refuse to sit on it, but will sell the jewels and distribute the money among the needy. Give him all the money America possesses, and he will certainly refuse to accept it, unless to be given away for a worthy cause for the uplift of humanity. His soul is perpetually anxious to give, and he expects absolutely nothing in return—not even thanks. This is no exaggeration, for I know him well: he came to our school at Bolpur and lived with us for some time. His power of sacrifice becomes all the more irresistible because it is wedded to his paramount fearlessness. Emperors and Maharajas, guns and bayonets, imprisonments and tortures, insults and injuries, even death itself, can never daunt the spirit of Gandhi. His is a liberated soul. If anyone strangles me, I shall be crying for help; but if Gandhi were strangled, I am sure he would not cry. He may laugh at his strangler; and if he has to die, he will die smiling. His simplicity of life is childlike, his adherence to truth is unflinching; his love for mankind is positive and aggressive. He has what is known as the Christ spirit. The longer I know him, the better I like him. It is needless for me to say that this great man is destined to play a prominent part in moulding the future of the world.'

'Such a great man deserves to be better known in the world. Why don't you make him known: you are a world figure?' I asked.

'How can I make him known? I am nothing compared to his illumined soul. And no truly great man has to be made great. They are great in their own glory, and when the world is ready they become famous by dint of their own greatness. When the time comes Gandhi will be known, for the world needs him and his message of love, liberty and brotherhood. The soul of the East has found a worthy symbol in Gandhi; for he is most eloquently proving that man is essentially a spiritual being, that he flourishes best in the realm of the moral and the spiritual, and most positively perishes, both body and soul, in the atmosphere of hatred and gunpowder smoke.'

1921

The Supreme Man

We have been waiting for the Person, such a personality as we see in Mahatma Gandhi. It is only possible in the East for such a man to become a great personality. He has neither physical nor material power, but through his great influence people who have been in subjection to all kinds of tyrannical power have stood up; and he is the strongest spiritual power in this world today. Not because of his political prudence, but for his spiritual influence the people believe in him, and they are ready to die for their faith. They are ready to suffer. It is a miracle that these people, downtrodden for centuries, are coming out; and without doing any injury to others they suffer, and through suffering, conquer.

And our women—only the other day they were secluded in their own inner apartments—they, too, have come out to follow this man, this leader. Not an association, not an organisation, not a politician, but a Man! And his message goes deep into our veins. He attacks the enemies that are within us. Not like the political machinery which you have that attacks from the outside and that tries to work through the external. But he attacks the inner man.

1 December 1930

Mahatma Gandhi

The geographical entity, that is India, appears from the earliest times to have roused in its people the desire to realise the unity comprised within its natural boundaries. In the *Mahabharata* we find the bringing together of its traditional memories scattered over different times and places; and, in the institution of systematic pilgrimages to the various sacred places dotted over its entire expanse, we discern the process of capturing a complete picture of its physical features within the net of a common devotion.

The old way had its merits. What was received naturally and directly penetrated deeper; and the arduous perambulation through the several centres of beauty and interest left an indelible impression.

From its place at the core of the *Mahabharata*, the Gita illuminated the synthesis thus achieved. From one point of view it may seem that the delivery of this philosophical discourse, standing on the brink of the Kurukshetra catastrophe, is out of place; whence it has come to be regarded as an interpolation. But, even so, the genius who later on placed it there knew that such a clarifying of fundamental issues at the heart of epic grandeur was necessary for the mind of India in order to gain a true vision of its essential wholeness, within and without.

And thus the reading of the *Mahabharata* was prescribed as a religious exercise for the people, not only because of the spiritual experiences it embodies, but also as a means of realising their own historical unity; and it was supplemented by the system of regular pilgrimages as affording intimate geographical contact with the country as a whole. So much for the plan of the sages of old.

When the Aryans, coming in through the western gate of India, first founded their colonies in the land of the five rivers and thence, over-passing the Vindhya range, gradually spread over the rest of the country, the whole of it, including adjoining provinces such as Gandhara, came under one and the same civilisation. One characteristic of this sameness was the recognition and acceptance of existing differences which, as it happened, led to their eventual perpetuation. But, though not tending to organic union, the coherence of the different elements was left undisturbed so long as a common consciousness of geographical solidarity remained vivid and unbroken by outside interference.

Then, through that same western gate, a succession of aggressors poured in with alien cultures, and therewith dawned the discovery that all this time we had merely been living together, but had not become one. The resulting weakness led to repeated floods of conquest, of the older people by neighbouring hordes, and of the latter, in turn, by distant exploiters from over the seas, none of them encountering any effective resistance to their advance.

In the disruption that ensued, internecine conflict became the order of the day, Indian contending against Indian for supremacy, or striving for ascendancy by temporary alliance with a foreign power. The history of India has since been, save for a brief interlude, one of suffering and progressive degradation, the depletion of its material resources bringing about mental and moral weakness; for poverty without ever results in poverty within. And it took us long centuries to realise that all this was due to the one original imperfection, of our failure to achieve unity of the same order as the vastness of the country.

There were, of course, redeeming forces at work all along. Whether, if India had been spared aggression from without, the spirit of her culture would have evolved a deep and abiding unity of her people or not, certain it is that even in the darkest period of her history, when her culture and her freedom were suddenly invaded and trampled upon, India reacted in her old, slow and subtle manner. Faced with the virile challenge of Islam, she released a spirit of mysticism that, incorporating the best in Islam, turned the very challenge to a source of new strength. The wisdom of the mediaeval saints and mystics, both Hindu and Muslim, thus carried on the progress of the slow unifying influences which we noticed in the age of the *Mahabharata*. But though these saintly souls strove to revive the reality of the ancient culture by spiritual sādhanā, unfortunately, so far as the generality of the people were concerned, this merely begot in them a hankering for other-worldly gains, leaving their destitution of body and mind in this world unremedied. Indeed, far from checking the wastage of their resources, this only aggravated it by what they poured into the bulging paunches of their religious exploiters.

Wandering amongst the teeming populace of India, there is now an increasing number of mendicant ascetics who leave the world around them to its penury and suffering, taking refuge in the aloofness of self-centred spiritual practices. I once had a few words with such a sannyāsi in some village. 'Why don't you,' I asked him, 'try to do something for these unfortunate villagers, afflicted with hunger, disease and wrong-doing?' He was both surprised and annoyed at my question. 'What!' he exclaimed, 'I who have shaken off the toils of worldly life for attaining pure bliss, am I again to entangle myself in the concerns of these bemused worldlings, labouring under their illusions?'

While India lay thus cramped and divided, betrayed by its own idealism, it was called upon to meet the greatest trial in her history—the challenge of Western imperialism. For the Aryans and the Muslims may have deprived a few Dravidian and Hindu dynasties of their rule in India, but they settled down among the people and their achievements became India's heritage. But here was a new impersonal empire, where the rulers were over us but not among us, who owned our land but could never belong to it. Never was India exposed to such relentless exploitation and subjected to such disintegration. The organic unity of Hindu culture was breaking down under Western influences, revealing the terrible cancer of untouchability. The Hindus and Muslims, despairing of their national good, began to quarrel among each other for scraps of patronage judiciously thrown out by the rulers. So disintegrated and demoralised had we become that many wondered if India could ever rise again by the genius of her own people, until there came on the scene a truly great soul, a great leader of men, in line with the tradition of the great sages of old, whom we are today assembled to honour—Mahatma Gandhi. Today no one need despair of the future of this country, for the unconquerable spirit that creates has already been released. Mahatma Gandhi has shown us a way by following which we shall not only save ourselves but may help other people also to save themselves.

He who has come to us today is, above all, distinguished by his freedom from any bias of personal or national selfishness. For the selfishness of the Nation can be a grandly magnified form of that same vice: the viciousness is there all the same. The standard of conduct followed by the class called politicians is not one of high ideals. They reck nothing of uttering falsehoods, they have no compunction in vitally hurting other people for the aggrandisement of their own. So we see in the West the spectacle of its nationals, on the one hand, freely giving up their lives for their country and, on the other, assisting it in all kinds of criminal activity, so much so that serious doubts have arisen as to how much longer this European civilisation will survive: the very thing they call patriotism bids fair to make an end of it. And, when the end comes, they will not meet it passively as our countrymen might have done, but to the accompaniment of all the horrors of a catastrophic upheaval.

Politicians plume themselves on being practical, and do not hesitate to ally themselves with the forces of evil, if they think that evil will accomplish their end. But tactics of this kind will not pass the audit of the Dispenser of our fortunes; so while we may admire their cleverness, we cannot revere them. Our reverence goes out to the Mahatma whose striving has ever been for Truth; who, to the great good fortune of our country at this time of its entry into the New Age, has never, for the sake of immediate results, advised or condoned any departure from the standard of universal morality.

He has shown the way how, without wholesale massacre, freedom may be won. There are doubtless but few amongst us who can rid our minds of a reliance on violence, who can really believe that victory may be ours without recourse to it. For even in the *Mahabharata*, not to speak of the 'civilised' warfare of the West, we find even dharma-yuddha to be full of violence and cruelty. Now, for the first time, perhaps, it has been declared that it is for us to yield up life, not to kill, and yet we shall win! A glorious message, indeed, not a counsel of strategy, not a means to a merely political end. In the course of unrighteous battle, death means extinction; in the non-violent battle of righteousness, something remains over—after defeat victory, after death immortality. The Mahatma, who has realised this in his own life, compels our belief in this truth.

As before, the genius of India has taken from her aggressors the most spiritually significant principle of their culture and fashioned of it a new message of hope for mankind. There is in Christianity the great doctrine that God became man in order to save humanity by taking the burden of its sin and suffering on Himself, here in this very world, not waiting for the next. That the starving must be fed, the ragged clad, has been emphasised by Christianity as by no other religion. Charity, benevolence, and the like, no doubt, have an important place in the religions of our country as well, but there they are in practice circumscribed within much narrower limits, and are only partially inspired by love of man. To our great good fortune, Gandhiji was able to receive this teaching of Christ in a living way. It was fortunate that he had not to learn Christianity from professional missionaries, but should have found in Tolstoy a teacher who had realised the value of non-violence through the multifarious experiences of his own life's struggles. For it was this great gift from Europe that our country had all along been awaiting.

In the middle ages also we had received gifts from Muslim sources. Dadu, Kabir and other saints had proclaimed that purity and liberation are not for being hoarded up in any temple, but are wealth to which all humanity is entitled. We should have no hesitation in admitting freely that this message was inspired by contact with Islam. The best of men always accept the best teaching, whenever and wherever it may be found, in religion, moral culture, or in the lives of individuals. But the middle ages are past, and we have stepped into a New Age. And now the best of men, Mahatma Gandhi, has come to us with this best of the gifts from the West.

But though Christ declared that the meek shall inherit the earth, Christians now aver that victory is to the strong, the aggressive. And no wonder. For the doctrine seemed, on the face of it, absurd and contrary to the principles of Natural History as interpreted by Western scientists. It needed another prophet to vindicate the truth of this paradox and interpret 'meekness' as the positive force of love and righteousness, as Satyagraha. This meekness is not submission, or mere passive endurance of wrong or injustice: such submission would be cowardly and would imply co-operation, even though involuntary, with the power of tyranny. But Gandhiji has made of this meekness, or ahimsā, the highest form of bravery, a perpetual challenge to the insolence of the strong.

It is difficult to say which of these contrary principles will eventually prevail. For arduous indeed is the quest of righteousness, while we are beset with the battling forces of evil around and within us. But whether any one of us is or is not capable of rising to the highest level of ahimsā, accept it, believe in it, we must; for have we not before us a man who, in the very thick of this modern age, by his own life and example, holds aloft this standard for us to follow? And while we pursue the path, with such slow steps as we may, the Mahatma's message will gradually become real for us. This day, therefore, is a memorable day, and on every return of it, year after year, for many a long year, and more and more vividly as the years go by, must we continue to remember his message.

2 October 1937

Gandhi the Man

After my return to India from some months' touring in the West, I found the whole country convulsed with the expectation of an immediate independence—Gandhiji had promised Swaraj in one year—by the help of some process that was obviously narrow in its scope and external in its observance.

Such an assurance, coming from a great personality, produced a frenzy of hope even in those who were ordinarily sober in their calculation of worldly benefits; and they angrily argued with me that in this particular case it was not a question of logic, but of a spiritual phenomenon that had a mysterious influence and miraculous power of prescience. This had the effect of producing a strong doubt in my mind about Mahatmaji's wisdom in the path he chose for attaining a great end through satisfying an inherent weakness in our character, which has been responsible for the age-long futility of our political life.

We, who often glorify our tendency to ignore reason, installing in its place blind faith, valuing it as spiritual, are ever paying for it with the obscuration of our mind and destiny. I blamed Mahatmaji for exploiting this irrational force of credulity in our people, which might have had a quick result in a superstructure, while sapping the foundation. Thus began my estimate of Mahatmaji, as the guide of our nation, and it is fortunate for me that it did not end there.

Gandhiji, like all dynamic personalities, needed a vast medium for the proper and harmonious expression of his creative will. This medium he developed for himself when he assumed the tremendous responsibility of leading the whole country to freedom past countless social ditches and fences, and the unlimited dullness of barren politics. This endeavour has enriched and mellowed his personality and revealed what was truly significant in his genius. I have since learnt to understand him, as I would understand an artist, not by the theories and fantasies of the creed he may profess, but by that expression in his practice which gives evidence to the uniqueness of his mind. In that only true perspective, as I watch him, I am amazed at the effectiveness of his humanity.

An ascetic himself, he does not frown at the joys of others, but works for the enlivening of their existence day and night. He exalts poverty in his own life, but no man in India has striven more assiduously than he for the material welfare of his people. A reformer with the zeal of a revolutionary, he imposes severe restraints on the very passions he provokes. Something of an idolator and also an iconoclast, he leaves the old gods in their dusty niches of sanctity and simply lures the old worship to better and more humane purposes. Professing his adherence to the caste system, he launches his firmest attack against it where it keeps its strongest guards, and yet he has hardly suffered from popular disapprobation as would have been the case with a lesser man who would have much less power to be effective in his efforts.

He condemns sexual life as inconsistent with the moral progress of man, and has a horror of sex as great as that of the author of *The Kreutzer Sonata*, but, unlike Tolstoy, he betrays no abhorrence of the sex that tempts his kind. In fact, his tenderness for woman is one of the noblest and most consistent traits of his character, and he counts among the women of his country some of his best and truest comrades in the great movement he is leading.

He advises his follower to hate evil without hating the evil-doer. It sounds an impossible precept, but he has made it as true as it can be made in his own life. I had once occasion to be present at an interview he gave to a certain prominent politician, who had been denounced by the official Congress party as a deserter. Any other Congress leader would have assumed a repelling attitude, but Gandhiji was all graciousness and listened to him with patience and sympathy, without once giving him occasion to feel small. Here, I said to myself, is a truly great man, for he is greater even than the creed he professes.

This, then, seems to me to be the significant fact about Gandhiji. Great as he is as a politician, as an organiser, as a leader of men, as a moral reformer, he is greater than all these as a man, because none of these aspects and activities limits his humanity. They are rather inspired and sustained by it. Though an incorrigible idealist, and given to referring all conduct to certain pet formulae of his own, he is essentially a lover of men and not of mere ideas; which make him so cautious and conservative in his revolutionary schemes. If he proposes an experiment for society, he must first subject himself to its ordeal. If he calls for a sacrifice, he must first pay its price himself. While many Socialists wait for all to be deprived of their privileges before they would part with theirs, this man first renounces before he ventures to make any claim on the renunciation of others.

There are patriots in India, as indeed among all people, who have sacrificed for their country as much as Gandhiji has done, and some who have had to suffer much worse penalties than he has ever had to endure; even as in the religious sphere, there are ascetics in this country, compared to the rigours of whose practices Gandhiji's life is one of comparative ease. But these patriots are mere patriots and nothing more; and these ascetics are mere spiritual athletes, limited as men by their very virtues; while this man seems greater than his virtues, great as they are.

Perhaps none of the reforms with which his name is associated was originally his in conception.

They have almost all been proposed and preached by his predecessors or contemporaries. Long before the Congress adopted them, I had myself preached and written about the necessity of a constructive programme of rural reconstruction in India; of handicrafts as an essential element in the education of our children; of the absolute necessity of ridding Hinduism of the nightmare of untouchability. Nevertheless, it remains true that they have never had the same energising power in them as when he took them up; for now they are quickened by the great life-force of the complete man who is absolutely one with his ideas, whose visions perfectly blend with his whole being.

His emphasis on the truth and purity of the means, from which he has evolved his creed of non-violence, is but another aspect of his deep and insistent humanity; for it insists that men in their fight for their claims must only so assert their rights, whether as individuals or as groups, as never to violate their fundamental obligation to humanity, which is to respect life. To say that because existing rights and privileges of certain classes were originally won and are still maintained by violence, and so they can only be destroyed by violence, is to create an unending circle of viciousness; for there will always be men with some grievance, fancied or real, against the prevailing order of society, who will claim the same immunity from moral obligation and the right to wade to their goal through slaughter. Somewhere the circle has to be broken, and Gandhiji wants his country to win the glory of first breaking it.

Perhaps he will not succeed. Perhaps he will fail as the Buddha failed and as Christ failed to wean men from their iniquities, but he will always be remembered as one who made his life a lesson for all ages to come.

January 1938

Mohandas Karamchand Gandhi

Today all of us who live in the āsram will joyfully celebrate Mahatma Gandhi's birthday. I want to indicate the spirit, the mood, to which the whole function is to be attuned.

In modern times such festivals have, to a great extent, become things of use and wont, lacking the proper inner urge. There is in them an element of pastime or recreation and of excitement. On account of these disturbing elements, the opportunity of receiving into the mind the deep significance of such occasions is dissipated.

Men of auspicious birth do not belong merely to the present. If their present roles must be made fully to represent them, then their personality has to be made smaller than it is. In this way we belittle the deathless personalities which stand out in perspective against the background of eternity. We pass the final judgment on their greatness, according to the standard of our immediate requirements. God wipes out from the picture which forms on the canvas of eternity the inevitable crooked and unconnected lines of the self-conflict and self-cancelment of daily life, and obliterates that which is accidental and transient; and thus a perfect, synthesised and compact image of those who are worthy of our reverence comes to live for ever. The value of festive functions like this lies in trying to look at our contemporaries also in this way.

India's political conflict of today may cease day after tomorrow; the purposes of our day, too, may be swept away in the current of time, nobody knows where. Let us assume that our political endeavour has been successful, that there is nothing for us to expect from outside, that India has obtained liberation. Nevertheless, what individual item of self-expression of the history of today will remain lifting up its head above the dust in spite of its downward drag—that alone is worthy of special consideration. It is when we think in that way that we understand what is the place, what the distinctiveness of him, who is the subject of our joyous celebration today. We will not prize him only for his achievement of our political ends: we will realise the greatness of that force by which he has today made the whole of India powerfully self-conscious.

Mighty is this force—it has today lifted from the breast of the country the heavy weight of inertness. In the course of a few years, India has obtained, as it were, a new birth—undergone a metamorphosis. Before his advent, fear covered the face of the land like a mantle—it remained overwhelmed with diffidence. There was only petitioning and appeal for others' favour, and the penury born of that want of faith in ourselves which lay embedded in the marrow of our bones.

The influence of those who are mere intruders from outside India is alone to be potent, while the current of India's life and consciousness, which has for ages run through her history, is to pale into insignificance as if it were accidental—what can be a sadder plight than this? We have really become outlanders because we have been prevented from intimately realising our motherland as ours by service, knowledge and loving neighbourliness. The administrative machinery and constitutional arrangements are the rulers. With their swords and firearms they are the principals in India, and we are secondary and subsidiary. Up till very recently our acquiescence in this, in our deluded state of mind, had kept all of us intellectually inert in the darkness of ignorance. At times some brave souls like Lokamanya Tilak have struck blows at this inertness, staking their lives in the venture, and have made it their mission to awaken the ideal of faith in the self. But Mahatma Gandhi has applied this ideal powerfully and on a vast scale in the field of action. Realising in his soul the genius of India, he has descended into the arena to make a new epoch with the unequalled power of his tapasyā. Now has commenced in our country, in a fitting manner, the campaign of fearless self-expression.

The foreign merchant-raj hitherto carried on the trade of imperialism, building its citadel on the foundation of our couragelessness. Armaments and armies would not have got enough room to take their stand upon, if our weakness had not given them shelter. We have supplied from within ourselves the greatest of the elements of our defeat. Mahatmaji has delivered us from this self-made defeat of ours. He has made the floods of consciousness of the new heroism flow in India. Now the rulers have become ready to enter into compromise with us, because the deepest foundation of their other-rule has been shaken, the foundation that was in our lack of heroism. We now easily demand our place in world society.

The man who has in England joined in the war of argumentation in the Round Table Conference, who has preached khaddar, who believes or does not believe in the prevalent science of medicine and in scientific machinery—we must know that we should not look upon that great person as bounded within his opinions and methods of work. He may err in the affairs of the times with which he is connected, there may be difference of opinion about them, but these are externals. Again and again he has admitted that he was mistaken; with changing times he has had to change his opinions. But the firm adherence to truth which has given his whole life an unshakable foundation—this unconquerable resolve was born with him—it is natural like the armour of Karna. The manifestation of this power is an everlasting treasure in human history. In the world of changing needs, the stream of continuous change flows on. But the glory of a great life which has today been revealed to our gaze, transcending all these needs—may we learn to respect that greatness.

This spirit of Mahatmaji's life has been infused into the whole country. It is chasing away our faintness. It is this figure of Gandhi the sādhaka, effulgent with this spirit, which stands on the pedestal of eternity. He has not allowed obstacles and dangers to stand in his way; his own mistakes have not dwarfed him; in the midst of the excitement of the hour, his mind, rising above it, yet retains its calm power of judgment. The man in whom resides this vast strength of character—it is him we salute on his birthday.

It is not the distinctive quality of man to be a mere repetition of his ancestors. Animals cling to the nests of their effete habits; man expresses himself age after age in new creations. Time-worn ideas can never keep him in their bondage. Let it be our sādhanā, our strenuous endeavour, to strengthen in *all* directions the spirit of rebellion roused by Mahatmaji in one direction against India's blindness and foolish custom of ages. Who has the power to liberate us so long as we are turned round and round in the whirlpool of caste, religious conflict, and foolish superstition? No nation can obtain deliverance from its woeful plight by strength of votes and the hair-splitting calculation of the respective rights of its constituent parts. The people, the foundation of whose society is full of cracks owing to internal strifes and restrictions; who go about carrying heaps of refuse in their almanacs; who with minds devoid of discrimination because of ignorance, rush to wash away their accumulated sins of generations in particular waters at particular auspicious moments; who fondly cherish the self-abasement of their intellects and powers, given in the name of infallible scriptures—such a people can never permanently and with the depth of realisation keep up that sādhanā, that strenuous endeavour which can sever the bonds of inner and outward servitude to others and can preserve with steadfast strength the heavy responsibilities of freedom against the onslaughts of all enemies. It must be borne in mind that the supreme test of manhood lies in battling against inner enemies; heroism of such high quality is not required in fighting external foes. He whom we honour today has victoriously stood this test. If the country does not accept from him the sādhanā for obtaining victory in that hard fight, then all our eulogies of him and all our festive prepartions would be in vain. Our sādhanā has only just begun; the path, beset with dangers and difficulties, lies ahead.

2 October 1931

20 September

A shadow is darkening today over India like a shadow cast by an eclipsed sun. The people of a whole country is suffering from a poignant pain of anxiety, the universality of which carries in it a great dignity of consolation. Mahatmaji, who through his life of dedication has made India his own in truth, has commenced his vow of extreme self-sacrifice.

Each country has its own inner geography where her spirit dwells and where physical force can never conquer even an inch of ground. Those rulers who come from outside remain outside the gate, and directly they are called away from the cloud-topping tower of their foreign possessions; the stupendous fabric of unreality vanishes into the void. But the great soul who achieves victory through the power of truth continues his dominion even when he is physically no longer present. And we all know such achievement belongs to Mahatmaji. And the fact that he has staked his life for a further and final realisation of his hope fills us with awe and makes us think.

At this solemn moment we have a cause for fear. It is our unfortunate habit to reduce the truth that belongs to the inner spirit into signs and observances that are external, and after a cheap welcome to bid it adieu. Our leaders have requested us to observe fasting for this day, and there is no harm in it. But there is the risk of some unthinking people putting it in the same category with the fasting that Mahatmaji has begun to observe. Nothing can be more disastrous for us than the utter lessening of the value of a heroic expression of truth by paying it the homage of a mere ceremonial expression of feeling by a people emotionally inclined.

The penance which Mahatmaji has taken upon himself is not a ritual, but a message to all India and to the world. If we must make that message our own, we should accept it in the right manner through a proper process of realisation. The gift of sacrifice has to be received in a spirit of sacrifice.

Let us try to understand the meaning of his message. From the beginning of human history there has continued the cleavage between classes, those favoured by circumstances exploiting the weakness of others and building the stronghold of their own pride of superiority upon the humiliation of a large section of the community. Though this practice has been prevalent for long, yet we must assert that it is against the true spirit of man. No civilised society can thrive upon victims whose humanity has been permanently mutilated, whose minds have been compelled to dwell in the dark. Those whom we keep down inevitably drag us down and obstruct our movement in the path of progress. The indignity with which we burden them grows into an intolerable burden to the whole country; we insult our own humanity by insulting Man where he is helpless or where he is not of our own kin.

Today there are thousands in India, confined in prisons indefinitely and without trial, inhumanly treated, and there can be no doubt that not only are they a heavy burden upon the Government but they permanently lower its dignity. The contemptuous vindictiveness ruthlessly pursued against prisoners, whether political or belonging to other classes, reveals the primitive barbarism lurking in the dark recesses of civilisation, perpetually burdening it with hard problems and tainting its soul. We, on our part in India, have banished a considerable number of our own people into a narrow enclosure of insult, branding them with the sign of permanent degradation. A dungeon does not solely consist of brick and mortar confinement, but setting narrow limits to man's self-respect is a moral prison more cruel for victims than the physical, one and more demoralising for those who encourage it passively or with pious fervour.

The concrete fact of inequalities between individuals and races cannot be ignored, but to accept it as absolute and utilise it to deprive men of their human rights and comradeship is a social crime that multiplies fast in its heinousness. We who imagine ourselves superior to those whom we have tied down to their abasement are punished by enfeebling them and losing them from amongst us. The weakness engendered by such alienation has been one of the principal causes of defeat in all our historical conflicts. Where numerous divisions have been made among the people by dark gaps of dishonour, balance is upset and the social structure is ever in danger of toppling over. The signs of such trials are not lacking in the Western continents, where the chasm between wealth and want is widening and is darkly nourishing earthquakes in its depth. The moral channels of communication should never be obstructed if man must be saved from degeneracy or destruction.

Mahatmaji has repeatedly pointed out the danger of those divisions in our country that are permanent insults to humanity, but our attention has not been drawn to the importance of its removal with the same force as it has been to the importance of khaddar. The social inequities in which all our enemies find their principal support have our time-honoured loyalty, making it difficult for us to uproot them. Against that deep-seated moral weakness in our society Mahatmaji has pronounced his ultimatum, and though it may be our misfortune to lose him in the battlefield, the fight will be passed on to every one of us to be carried on to the final end. It is the gift of the fight which he is going to offer to us, and if we do not know how to accept it humbly and yet with proud determination, if we cheaply dismiss it with some ceremonials to which we are accustomed and allow the noble life to be wasted, with its great meaning missed, then our people will passively roll down the slope of degradation to the blankness of utter futility.

It is not possible for us to realise what effect Mahatmaji's action will have upon the people who govern us, and it is not for us today to discuss its political aspects.

Only one thing we must make clear to those who seem to have our destiny in their hands. We have observed that the English people are puzzled at the step that Mahatmaji has been compelled to take. They confess that they fail to understand it. I believe that the reason of their failure is mainly owing to the fact that the language of Mahatmaji is fundamentally different from their own. His method of protest is not in accord with the method which they usually follow in cases of grave political crisis. I may remind them of the inhuman atrocities and bloodshed of those terrible days when Ireland was trying to break free from the rest of Great Britain. Those Englishmen who imagined it to be disastrous to the integrity of their Empire did not scruple to kill and be killed, even to tear into shreds the decency of civilised codes of honour. The West is accustomed to such violent outbursts in times of desperation, and therefore such a procedure did not seem strange to them, though to some of them it must have appeared wrong. The dismemberment of a large portion of Hindu society is certainly fatal to its wholeness, and the reason should not be incomprehensible to other people as to why Mahatmaji is voicing the extreme form of protest on behalf of India. I ask them to imagine what would have happened when the Roman Catholic community of England suffered a forcible deprivation of its common rights, if some foreign power had come and with efficient benevolence alienated them from the rest of the nation. Very likely the people would have resorted to the method of protest which they consider honourable in its red fury of violence. In our case the feeling may be similar, though Mahatmaji has given it an expression which is his own. The message of non-violence so often expressed by him in words and in deeds finds today its final exposition in a great language which should be easiest to understand.

20 September 1932

With Mahatmaji in Poona

We left for Poona with hope in our hearts even though the atmosphere was tense with foreboding. The journey was long, giving time for anxious thoughts to dwell on what may await us at the end. My companions bought newspapers at every big railway stall—the news was not encouraging. Mahatmaji, according to the physicians, seemed to have definitely entered the danger zone, his muscles yielding now that his naturally meagre surplus of fat had almost been exhausted. Apoplexy might result any time. Discussions with different groups, prolonged and intricate, continued all these days mercilessly to exact his best energies. And yet Mahatmaji had indeed triumphed, curbing intense physical agony and mental strain with an unbending will. Compromise seemed to have been achieved, retaining the depressed communities within the Hindu fold, and frustrating attempts to create divisions by the separate electorate award. The final resolution was now with the British Cabinet, though there was no reasonable ground for their withholding sanction as the Prime Minister had already committed himself to the acceptance of what our own communities may jointly recognise as just.

Wavering between hope and fear, we reached Kalyan on the morning of 26 September. We met Srimati Basanti and Urmila on the platform—they had arrived some hours before by the B.N.R. Mail. Without delay we started for Poona by the car which our hostess there had sent for us.

The hilly road through the Western Ghats is picturesque. Entering the city of Poona we found armoured cars and machine guns being manoeuvred on the military grounds; soldiers paraded along the city roads. Lady Thackersay herself graciously received us at her doorstep; as we went up the stairs to our rooms, the girls of her school standing on either side welcomed us with songs and ceremonial garlands, and sandal-paste.

Entering the house I sensed anxiety in the air; there was a shadow of suspense on every face. On questioning I found that Mahatmaji's condition was precarious. No answer had come from London. I sent an urgent cable to the Premier.

There was no need for sending it. Soon the rumour reached us that the expected news had arrived. But we had no means of verifying that rumour till many hours later.

It was Mahatmaji's day of silence. He had expressed the desire that I should be with him when he broke his silence at one o'clock. On our way to the Yeravda prison, at some distance from the gate our car was stopped—a sentry on duty had been asked not to let any car pass till further orders. I had thought that in India nowadays the road to the jail entrance is wide open. Round our car gathered a medley crowd.

As a gentleman from our side proceeded to obtain sanction from the prison authorities, Sriman Devadas came along in a car, the jail-permit in his hand. Later on I heard that Mahatmaji had suddenly felt that our car had been obstructed on the way—though he had no information on that point—and sent his son to fetch us.

Big iron doors swung wide open one after the other and closed behind us. To our front was the arrogance of high walls, a fettered sky, straight-cut metalled roads projecting ahead, a few trees.

Two major experiences of my life have come rather late. Recently I had crossed the threshold of the University; and inspite of a slight obstruction, here was I today inside a regular prison house.

Climbing a few steps to the left and passing through a door I entered a walled-in enclosure with two blocks of cells, some distance apart. In the middle courtyard, under the thick shade of a young mango tree, lay Mahatmaji on his bed.

Mahatmaji drew me near to himself, and kept me there for some time. 'What a joy it is to see you,' he said.

I praised my luck for having come on the crest of good news. It was nearly half past one. The message from London had by now spread all over India, and it had even been discussed at the Assembly—so I heard later. The newspapermen had also known of it. There seemed only to have been no hurry in saving him whose life-stream hour by hour was rapidly dwindling to vanishing point. One felt surprised at the cruelly tortuous length of Red Tape. Up to four in the afternoon our anxiety mounted higher. One hears that the information had arrived in official Poona at 10 a.m.

On all sides were friends. I recognised among them Mahadev, Vallabhbhai, Rajagopalachari, Rajendraprasad. Srimati Kasturibai and Sarojini as well as Jawaharlal's wife, Kamala, were there.

Mahatmaji's slender body was emaciated to a degree, his voice was barely audible. He was being given water with soda to counteract the growing acidity in his stomach. The responsibility of his physicians was grave.

Yet his inner vigour was undiminished, his intellect active, his radiant personality as ever tireless. From before his fast difficult problems had weighed on his mind; he had carried on intricate discussions; his correspondence with politicians across the seas must have been a strenuous experience. During his fast, as every one knows, the claims and clamour of different parties have not spared him. Not a sign, however, of mental fatigue, not the slightest shadow was there to obscure the lucid language of his thoughts. Transcending the extreme rigours of his body, this great manifestation of his invincible soul was before us, moving us to profound admiration. I could hardly have fully realised how great is the strength of this frail man had I not come near to him like this.

Today, to millions of hearts in India has reached the message of this immortal spirit resting under the shadow of death's altar. No barriers could stand in its way—of distance, of brick and mortar, or of hostile politics. The obstruction of century-old inertia had crumbled before it into dust.

Mahadev said that Mahatmaji had been eagerly awaiting my arrival. I cannot offer any help in the solution of political problems, for I lack necessary experience and inclination; but I am happy to have given him some satisfaction by my personal presence.

We moved on to a distance as it would tire him to be surrounded. We patiently waited for the message to arrive. The afternoon light arched over the bare high walls. In groups, white khaddar-clothed men and women quietly held discussions. Noticeable was the disciplined calm of this gathering inside the jail. No hint was there of unguarded behaviour taking advantage of relaxed regulations. This strength of character naturally evokes trust, the prison authorities therefore have respectfully allowed them unhampered to mix with each other. They have not accepted any privileges transgressing Mahatmaji's implied assurance to the authorities. The dignity of natural self-respect is theirs; one can easily understand that they fully deserve the responsibility which rests on them to establish India's Swaraj on unflinching service of Truth.

At last, with the Government's red-sealed envelope in hand, appeared the Inspector-General of Prisons. There seemed to be a hint of happiness on his face. Slowly Mahatmaji read the document. I asked Sarojini to request others to move away from him now. After he had finished reading, Mahatmaji called his friends to discuss the communication amongst themselves and expressed his wish that it should be shown to Dr Ambedkar.

This letter was pondered over; I too read it. A production of diplomatic minds, it needed careful perusal. One understood that it did not go against Mahatmaji's wishes. Pandit Hridaynath Kunzru was deputed to explain the document in detail to Mahatmaji. His clear analysis left no room for doubt in Mahatmaji's mind. The great penance of the fast was now over.

Mahatmaji's cot was removed near to the shade of the prison wall. Spreading the jail blankets, the gathering was seated. The lemon juice was prepared by Srimati Kamala Nehru; according to the request of the Inspector-General of Prisons, it was to be given to Mahatmaji by Srimati Kasturibai. Mahadev told me that my Gitanjali song 'When the heart is dried and parched up' is a favourite of Mahatmaji's. I had forgotten the tune which once I gave it; I sang it to an improvised tune. Pandit Syam Sastri read out from the Vedas. Srimati Kasturibai handed to Mahatmaji the glass of fruit juice which he took and slowly sipped. Then the members of Sabarmati ?sram and others sang in chorus the hymn 'Vaishnava Jana Ko'. Fruits and sweets were distributed, we all partook of them.

Within gaol barricades this great festival took place. Never had happened such an event in human history. The yajna (sacrificial rite) was begun inside the prison and it was here that it reached its great fulfilment.

At night Pandit Kunzru and other notable leaders, now assembled in Poona, came to me with the request that I should preside at the mammoth meeting to be held tomorrow to celebrate Mahatmaji's birthday anniversary. Pandit Malaviya, they said, would arrive tomorrow from Bombay. Panditji, I proposed, should preside; I would read out a short address in which I would try adequately to express my own sentiments. It was impossible not to consent to join even a big gathering on an occasion so auspicious, overruling considerations of my age and health.

Next evening, in the open grounds of Sivaji Mandir a vast gathering met to do honour to their master. With difficulty I entered, wondering how I would ever manage to come out. Malaviyaji in his chaste Hindi explained beautifully that our scriptures never support class or racial discrimination in the name of religion; quoting chapter and verse he proved his thesis. I knew it was impossible for my voice any more to make itself audible to a meeting of this size. So I spoke a few words; Sriman Govind Malaviya, son of Panditji, undertook to read out the text of my address. It was surprising to find that he could do it so perfectly, considering that the evening light was dim and that he saw the paper now for the first time.

My written speech has already appeared fully in the papers. Just before coming to the meeting I had gone to Yeravda prison and presented it to Mahatmaji.

Mrs Motilal Nehru, addressing her brothers and sisters, said that they should never pause in their fight against untouchability, which was a blot on the fair name of our civilisation. Srijuts Rajagopalachari, Rajendraprasad, and other leaders exhorted their audience with great feeling to remove this evil which was disrupting our society and thwarting at every step our larger aspirations. Srijut Rajagopalachari wanted to take with him a birthday present for Mahatmaji in his jail. Let it be then the promise never again to tolerate untouchability in our lives. At the end of the meeting, the entire audience raising their hands accepted the vow of purging our social life of the grave wrongs that humiliate our humanity. It was evident that the message of today had reached the hearts of our audience—it would have been impossible even a few days before for thousands of men and women to accept unanimously such a difficult resolve.

My work was done. Next morning I spent many hours with Mahatmaji. Pandit Malaviya and myself had long discussions with him on a wide range of subjects. In a day Mahatmaji had regained unexpected physical strength, his voice was firmer, his blood pressure nearly normal. Visitors poured in with greetings of devoted love, to take the dust of his feet. He talked smilingly with each person. Children came with gifts of flowers. How happy he is with them! Discussions continued with his friends on social problems. His great concern now is to achieve harmony between our two great communities, the Hindus and Mahomedans.

His great life, which today luminously reveals itself on a large background, has brought to us the message of discovering man the great in all humanity. May this message be fulfilled. The true path to emancipation lies in man's unity; our political dependence is nourished by the innumerable sects and divisions that keep our people apart. The day has come when human civilisation must move forward, breaking through the fetters of the Ages— towards broader understanding based on mutual faith and love.

October 1932

On Mahatmaji's Birthday

Mahatmaji's birthday appears today before us in the awful majesty of death which has just left him victorious.

Ordinarily men are born to a limited neighbourhood where, related to their kinsmen, they carry on the course of their commonplace life till they die. Every year they also enjoy their special day which assures them of their birthright of a seat in the hearts of their few friends and relations. But great souls are born into a large sphere of life, they are acknowledged by people and nations: in celebrating their birthday we not only realise them to be our own for all time, but through them feel our spiritual intimacy with the world of man. They extend the range of our personal self, giving it a universal background, the significance of eternal humanity.

It is our great good fortune today that such a man has indeed come to us, and what is still rarer that we have not repudiated him as we have so often done the messengers of freedom and truth. His inspiration is actively in work all through India and even beyond its boundaries; it has awakened our consciousness to a truth which goes far beyond the limits of our self-interest. His life itself is a constant call to us, to emancipation in service and self-dedication.

Today is the day of our national acknowledgement of Mahatmaji as the great brother, who in the present age is the central bond of our brotherhood in our Motherland. I hope we shall be earnestly solemn in our expression of it and never cheapen the meaning of this occasion by merely indulging in emotional pride. Let us be worthy of the call of this Age and accept from Mahatmaji's hand the responsibility which he has accepted for himself.

We know in the Upanishads, God, who ever dwells in the hearts of all men, has been mentioned as Mahatma. The epithet is rightly given to the man of God whom we are honouring today, for his dwelling is not within the narrow enclosure of individual consciousness, his dwelling is in the heart of untold multitudes who are born today in India and who are yet to come. And this greatness of his soul, which has the power to comprehend other souls, has made possible what never has yet happened in our history when even the masses have been roused to the great fact that India is not merely a geographical entity but a living truth, in which they live and move and have their being.

Today in our determined effort to join Mahatmaji in his noble task of removing the burden of the Ages, the burden of disrespect upon the bent back of those who have been stigmatised for the accident of their birth, the sin of wilful denial to a large body of our countrymen of sympathy which is the birthright of all human beings—we are not only casting off the chain of India's moral enslavement, but indicating a path for all humanity. We are challenging victimisation, wherever and in whatever form it may exist, to stand the test of the relentless questioning of conscience which Mahatmaji has brought to bear upon our day.

When Mahatmaji began his penance, there were cynics in our own country and abroad who mocked and jeered at him. And yet before our very eyes the wonder has happened. Hard rocks of tradition have been blasted, irrational prohibitions cramping our national life are already showing signs of tottering. Great has been the achievement due to his penance, but it will be a greater glory to him and to us if we can fulfil his vow by fighting to the finish the evils of untouchability, of intolerance, of all that hinders the comradeship of man and man and obstructs our path to freedom and righteousness.

My friends, I appeal to you, do not betray your great man and your own humanity by any deviation of your initiative from the pursuit of justice and love towards your fellowmen, who have suffered humiliation for ages and remained dumb in a pathetic apathy of resignation, never even blaming Providence and their own cruel destiny. But the angry voice has at last come from the divine guide of our history with its warning message that they cut at the root of freedom who in their unreasoning pride obstruct the freedom of social communication among their own kindred.

27 September 1932

Moral Warfare

By segregating ethics to the Kingdom of Heaven, and depriving the Kingdom of Earth from its use, man has up to now never seriously acknowledged the need of higher ideals in politics or in practical affairs. That is why when disagreements occur between individuals, violence, is not encouraged but punished; but when the combatants are nations, barbaric methods are not only not condemned but glorified. The greatest of men like Buddha or Christ have from the dawn of human history stood for the ideal of non-violence; they have dared to love their enemies and defied tyranny by peace, but we have not yet claimed the responsibility they have offered us.

Fight is necessary in this world, combat we must, and relentlessly, against the evils that threaten us, for by tolerating untruth we admit their claim to exist.

But war on the human plane must be what in India we call dharma-yuddha—moral warfare; in it we must array our spiritual powers against the cowardly violence of evils. This is the great ideal which Mahatma Gandhi represents, challenging his people to fearlessly apply man's highest strength, not only in our individual dealings but in the clash of nation with nation.

In the barbaric age, man's hunger did not impose any limits on its range of food which included even human flesh, but with the evolution of society this has been banished from extreme possibility: in like manner we await the time when nothing may supposedly justify the use of violence, whatever consequences we are led to face. Because, success in a conflict may be terrible defeat from the human point of view, and material gain is not worth the price we pay at spiritual cost. Much rather should we lose all than barter our soul for an evil victory. We honour Mahatma Gandhi because he has brought this ideal into the sphere of politics, and under his lead India is proving every day how aggressive power pitifully fails when human nature in its wakeful majesty bears insult and pain without retaliating. India today, inspired by her great leader, opens the new chapter of human history which has just begun.

1930

References

This is principally a selection of Rabindranath Tagore's addresses on Mahatma Gandhi's birth anniversaries, and on the occasion of Mahatmaji's 'Epic Fast' in 1932.

- 'Gandhi Maharaj' is a translation of the Bengali poem, 'Gandhi Maharaj', and is reproduced from the *Visva-Bharati Quarterly*, February 1941.
- 'A Liberated Soul' is an interview granted to a press reporter during the poet's foreign tour in 1920–21.
- 'The Supreme Man' is an extract from a speech at a reception held under the auspices of the Discussion Guild and the Indian Society of America on 1 December 1930, reproduced here from the *Visva-Bharati Quarterly*, VIII, 1930–31, part III.
- 'Mahatma Gandhi' is an English version by Surendranath Tagore of an address delivered in Bengali

at Santiniketan on Mahatmaji's birthday, 2 October 1937. It was first published in the *Visva-Bharati Quarterly*, November 1937.

- 'Gandhi the Man' was contributed to *The Sunday Statesman*, 13 February 1938.
- 'Mohandas Karamchand Gandhi' is an English version of an address delivered in Bengali at Santiniketan on Mahatma Gandhi's birthday, 2 October 1931. It was first published in the *Modern Review*, January, 1932.
- '20 September' is the English version of an address delivered in Bengali at Santiniketan on the day Mahatmaji entered 'the fiery gate' of fasting.
- 'With Mahatmaji in Poona' is the English version of an account related by Rabindranath Tagore to the inmates of Santiniketan on his return from Poona, where he had proceeded to be with Mahatma Gandhi during his fast.
- 'On Mahatmaji's Birthday' is an address delivered at a public meeting held at Sivaji Mandir, Poona, on 27 September 1932.
- 'Moral Warfare' is a message to the Society of Friends.
- The three addresses—'Mahatma Gandhi', '20 September,' and 'With Mahatmaji in Poona'—are reproduced in this book from *Rabindranath Tagore: Mahatmaji and the Depressed Humanity* (1932).